Lions

Lions

by Sarah Albee

Reader's Digest.
YOUNG FAMILIES

Published by The Reader's Digest Association Limited
London • New York • Sydney • Montreal

CONTENTS

Chapter 1

Two cubs grow up

On a hot, windy day, a group of lions sit on the sun-baked grass of a wide-open African plain. But one lioness breaks away from the rest of the pride. She is looking for a safe place to have her babies.

The mother lion gives birth to two babies. They are tiny, blind and helpless, needing their mother for everything. They weigh just over 1 kilogram – little more than a bag of flour. It will be three weeks before they start to walk. Their mother feeds them and keeps them safe from hungry hyenas and leopards by moving them to different hiding places.

wildWORDS

pride   **a group of lions living together.**

A few months pass. Early one morning, Mother Lion kisses her cubs goodbye. She and the other females are going off to hunt. The cubs' aunt stays behind to watch out for all the babies in the pride.

A few hours later, the hunters return. They have not brought back any food this time. But they will try again tonight.

Just as she is about to lie down and rest with her cubs, Mother Lion leaps to her feet, growling. She has heard an unfamiliar roar. A male lion is nearby, ready to attack. If he tried to take over the pride, the cubs would be in danger.

While her cubs hide, she and the other adult females roar fiercely at the stranger. The cubs' father gets ready to fight him. The stranger changes his mind about attacking. He runs away. The pride is safe.

Do cubs hunt?

Cubs start hunting with their mothers when they are nearly a year old. But their mothers and other lions will still provide food for them until they are about two years old.

That evening, the cubs' mother goes hunting again. This time, she and the other hunters manage to kill a large animal. The pride eats well.

After the lions eat, they flop down under some trees to take a long nap.

As the years pass, the cubs grow up quickly. The male cub starts to grow hair around his head and neck — this is called a mane. Soon it will be time for him to leave this group to find his own pride and to mate. The female cub will stay in the pride with her mother and other female relatives for the rest of her life.

Him and her

Lions are the only type of big cat where the males and females look quite different.

Chapter 2

The body of a lion

DID YOU KNOW?

Your pet cat probably
purrs when it is happy.
Lions can also purr,
but they don't do it
often.

Big cats, small cats

Superb hearing

Lions can turn their ears in different directions to hear sounds from all around. They can hear an animal that is a mile away.

If you have a pet cat, you've probably noticed some interesting things about it. It has excellent eyesight and hearing. It moves gracefully — whether it is walking, running or leaping. It uses its long tail for balance. Your cat often grooms itself with its tongue. And it sleeps or rests a lot.

Now imagine a cat that does all these things but weighs perhaps 50 times as much — up to 225 kilograms — is 3 metres long from nose to tail and has a big mane — a male lion.

Female lions — lionesses — do not have manes and are smaller than the males. They are about 2 metres long and weigh about 135 kilograms.

Glorious manes

A male lion's mane starts to grow at the age of two or three and is fully grown when the lion is about five years old. The colour ranges from pale yellow to black, and the mane gets darker with age.

Some adult male lions have bigger manes than others. Lions with large manes are important and treated with respect. They often get to eat first and can scare their enemies easily. When a lion sees another lion with a large mane, it will often back off rather than attack him. While a mane may make a lion look big and frightening, luckily it's made of fluff so it isn't heavy.

The mane also protects the lion's head and neck from bites and scratches during fights with other animals.

Baby teeth

Like human children, lion cubs lose their baby teeth. They get their permanent teeth at about two years old. Some of their teeth can be 5 centimetres long – bigger than your little finger. An adult lion has 30 teeth.

DID YOU KNOW?

Lions have thick padding on the bottoms of their paws. These special pads help them move quietly and stop them from skidding on slippery surfaces.

Adult male lions are the only cats with a mane.

DID YOU KNOW?

Have you ever watched someone else yawn and then started to yawn yourself? The same thing happens to lions with yawning, grooming and roaring. If one does it, the rest of the pride follows.

Lions can leap an amazing distance in one bound – as far as 10 metres. Their strong muscles also allow them to capture an animal three times their size.

Lions in action

Lions can run, jump, pounce, climb trees and even swim if they have to. Like other cats, their backs are flexible. This flexibility, combined with their powerful leg muscles, means that lions can leap high in the air and land safely.

Lions also have excellent vision and hearing. They can see in the dark and their eyes are widely spaced so they can see things on each side as well as in front.

Cool cats

Lions like to rest during the day when the sun is hottest. Young lions climb trees where there are cooling breezes. Older, bigger lions look for a shady spot under trees. Sometimes lions lie on their backs to allow the air to cool their undersides.

Chapter 3

Lion families

Mothers, daughters, sisters and female cousins usually live in the same pride their whole lives. Males stay for only a few years.

DID YOU KNOW?

Lions are the only members of the cat family that work together to raise their young and to hunt for food.

A matter of pride

Why do lions live together in groups? Group living seems to benefit all the lions in the pride. They hunt for food together, groom one another, and take care of one another's babies.

There can be as many as 40 lions in a pride but big prides often split into smaller groups. A pride usually consists of two to 18 females and their offspring and one to seven males, with one male as the chief.

If another male challenges the chief lion, there is often a fight for control of the pride. The chief lion tends to be overthrown every three years or so.

The adult females in the group are in charge of caring for the cubs, finding water, deciding where the group will sleep, and hunting for food. If a mother lion dies, other females in the pride adopt her cubs.

When male cubs reach the age of about two or three, they are ready to leave the pride. For a time, they travel without a pride, sometimes in pairs, hunting on their own. Two brothers or male cousins will often remain together for life. When they are fully grown, they try to take control of another pride.

wild WORDS

simba **In Africa, this is the Swahili word for lion. It also means, 'strong' and 'king'.**

Heads and tails

How do lions announce their presence to others? One good way to get attention is to roar! Lions roar to let other lions of their pride know where they are. Males also roar to warn rivals to stay away from their territory, which can be as big as a city – covering about 100 to 130 square kilometres.

Another way lions warn other animals to stay away is by marking their territory. Male lions mark their territory by spraying a combination of urine and scent. The scent is made by special glands at the base of their tails. Lions put their scent at nose-level, so that other lions can easily detect the odour. They also scratch or claw marks on trees and other places as warnings.

Lions have very expressive faces. They use their facial expressions, as well as their bodies, to communicate. Lions commonly greet one another by head-rubbing and grooming.

DID YOU KNOW?

● Male lions that live in zoos also mark their territory. They have been known to back up to crowds and shoot a stream of marking scent as far as 3 or 4 metres. And often when one male lion does it, the rest of the males do it, too.

● Lions are the only members of the cat family with a tuft of fur at the end of their tails. They use it to communicate with each other. They can see each other's tails above the tall grass and know if another lion is cross or happy, depending on the way the tail moves.

The roar of a lion can sometimes be heard as far as 5 miles away.

Lion cubs love to play. Like young children, they try to get their parents' attention any way they can.

Playtime

Lion cubs spend a great deal of time playing together. They play-fight, chase one another and wrestle. Adults occasionally join in the play. A mother lion will flick her tail, allowing the cubs to pounce on it. Much of the cubs' play imitates skills they will use as adults, such as stalking and pouncing. Playing together is also an important way for cubs to bond with one another. Often they remain lifelong companions.

Keeping clean

Lions are careful groomers, keeping their front paws, manes and chests clean with their rough tongues. Lions groom both themselves and one another. Grooming other lions helps them to make friends and also to get rid of insects from each other's fur. A lion grooming itself licks in the same direction the fur grows, but another lion can lick the fur in the opposite direction.

Chapter 4

King of the beasts

A lion chasing down prey
can run the length of a
football pitch in 6 seconds.

Going on the hunt

In order to survive, lions spend a lot of their waking time hunting for food. Lions are carnivores, which means they eat other animals. Lions eat gnu, impalas, zebra, gazelles, buffalo, giraffes, wildebeest, antelope, wild boars and even young hippopotamuses. During hard times, lions eat practically anything – fish, snakes, fruit and even insects.

Because lionesses are smaller and faster than male lions, they are the ones that usually do the hunting for the pride. Lions hunt both in groups and alone.

Over time, lions have learned that they are more successful at catching very large prey when they hunt together. Usually one group of lions circles a potential victim and then stops in front of it. Meanwhile, another group of lions scares the prey from behind, forcing it to run right into the first group of lions.

Young male lions, alone or in pairs, also hunt. Even the chief male in a pride may join a hunt. Sometimes his greater size and strength are needed to bring down an animal that is much bigger than the females.

DID YOU KNOW?

● **Lions are at the very top of the food chain and all other animals tend to avoid them. The only enemies that pose a danger to lions are human beings with weapons.**

● **Lions are able to sprint as fast as 35 miles per hour – for short distances only. Most of the animals they chase can run a lot faster. So lions quietly creep up close to their prey – within 6 or 9 metres – and then dash out and leap onto their victim to try to overpower it.**

Table manners

Lion hunts are often unsuccessful. If a group of lion hunters can't catch its prey after a short chase, the lions give up because they are too tired to continue.

Sometimes it's easier to take another animal's food. When lions hear the sound of hyenas, wild dogs or even other large cats eating, they know where they can get a fast meal. Few animals are foolish enough to protest when hungry lions arrive and take away their dinner.

Animals that have died of natural causes are also food for lions. When lions see vultures circling in the air, it is a signal that a carcass is available.

Although females generally bring down prey, it's the males who tend to eat first. Occasionally the females can take a few bites before the males chase them away. When the male lions have finished eating, the females get their turn. Only then are the cubs and young lions allowed to eat. Some of the more aggressive cubs sneak in and eat with the males while the rest of the pride keeps a respectful distance.

An adult male lion can eat as much as 40 kilograms of meat in just one meal.

Lions rest and sleep a lot –
sometimes as much as
20 hours in a 24 hour day.

Big-cat naps

Lions do most of their hunting at night or very early in the morning, when the air is cooler. When they find food, lions gorge themselves, eating as much as they possibly can. They know from experience that it might be several days before they have another successful hunt and are able to eat again.

Lions like to take a nap after eating a large meal and they need the rest to conserve energy. Hunting is hard work.

Other animals often graze close to resting or sleeping lions and don't seem at all frightened or concerned. They appear to understand that lions who are resting out in the open are no threat to them.

Chapter 5

Lions in the world

savannah a hot
grassland area
with scattered
trees. It has two
seasons – a long
dry one when the
grass turns golden-
brown and a short
one with heavy
rains.

DID YOU KNOW?

Most lions live on
savannahs, but some
live in wooded areas
with open spaces.
Lions can even survive
in areas that suffer
from extreme drought,
such as desserts.

Lions are the light-brown
colour of sun-dried grass.
Their colour helps them
blend into their surroundings
and sneak up on their prey.

Lands of the Lions

PAST AND PRESENT

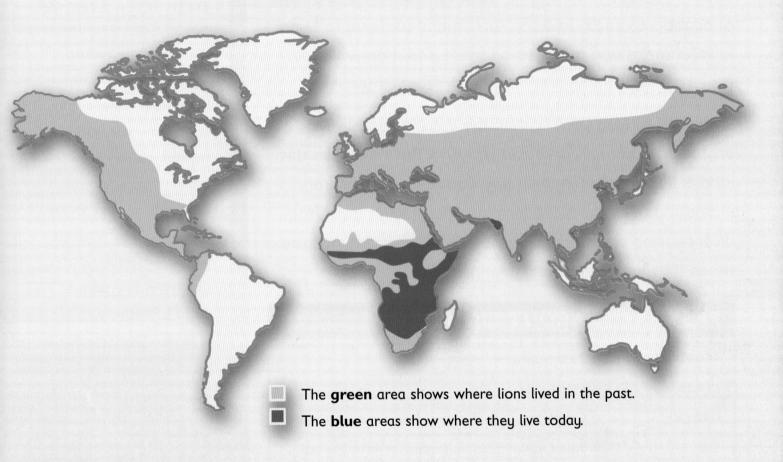

The **green** area shows where lions lived in the past.

The **blue** areas show where they live today.

Thousands of years ago, there were lions living in Europe, Asia and even in North America. But changes in the climate, hunting by humans and the growth of farms and cities have all enormously reduced the lions' territories. The number of lions has also decreased. Today almost all the world's lions live in Africa, though scientists are not quite sure how many. Some estimate that there are fewer than 50,000. A few hundred live in India.

The future of lions

To survive, lions need enough land to roam on and plenty of animals to catch and eat. As humans continue to build farms, houses and factories on more and more wild lands, the areas where lions can wander freely has shrunk.

Most of Africa's lions and all the lions in India live in protected national parks and reserves. But now even this land is being threatened by population growth and an increasing need for more farmland. To prevent lions from disappearing completely, it is important to safeguard the areas that have been set aside for them.

DID YOU KNOW?

All cats – including lions and your pet house cat – belong to the same scientific family, called *Felidae*. Lions, tigers, leopards and jaguars are even more closely related to one another and are from the genus called *Panthera*.

FAST FACTS ABOUT LIONS

SCIENTIFIC NAME	*Panthera leo*
CLASS	Mammals
ORDER	Carnivora
SIZE	Males about 2.4m in length, not including tail Females about 1.5m in length, not including tail
WEIGHT	Males to 225kg Females to 135kg
LIFE SPAN	About 15 years in the wild About 30 years in captivity
HABITAT	Savannahs and open wooded areas
TOP SPEED	35 miles per hour in short bursts

YOU CAN HELP!

Become a member of a conservation group that works to protect the habitats of lions. It may even be your local zoo.

GLOSSARY OF **Wild** WORDS

carcass	the body of a dead animal
carnivore	a meat-eating animal
conservation	the protection and preservation of land, animals, plants and other natural resources
cub	a young meat-eating mammal
drought	a long period of time without rain
ecosystem	all the living and non-living things in a certain environment

genus	a large category of related plants or animals consisting of smaller groups (species) of closely related plants or animals
grooming	cleaning of fur, skin or feathers by an animal
habitat	the natural environment where an animal or a plant lives
hyena	a meat-eating mammal that resembles a dog, found in Africa and Asia
mammal	an animal with a backbone and hair on its body that drinks milk from its mother when it is born

mane — long hair on the head or neck of an animal

plain — a large, flat area of land, usually without trees

predator — an animal that hunts and eats other animals to survive

prey — animals that are hunted by other animals for food

pride — a group of lions that live together

reserves — areas of land or water where plants and animals are protected

savannah — a flat grassland area with scattered trees in a hot region of the world

simba — the Swahili word for lion, strong and king

species — a group of plants or animals that are the same in many ways

territory — an area of land that an animal considers to be its own and will fight to defend

victim — a living thing that is hunted or killed

INDEX

CREDITS

Lions is an *All About Animals* fact book
published by Reader's Digest Young Families, Inc.

Written by Sarah Albee

Copyright © 2005 Reader's Digest Young Families, Inc.
This edition was adapted and published in 2008 by
The Reader's Digest Association Limited
11 Westferry Circus, Canary Wharf, London E14 4HE

® Reader's Digest, the Pegasus logo and Reader's Digest Young Families
are registered trademarks of
The Reader's Digest Association, Inc.

We are committed to both the quality of our products and the service we provide to our customers.
We value your comments, so please feel free to contact us on
08705 113366 or via our website at: www.readersdigest.co.uk
If you have any comments or suggestions about the content of our books,
you can contact us at: gbeditorial@readersdigest.co.uk

Printed in China

Book code: 640-001 UP0000-1
ISBN: 978 0 276 44318 3